COPTIC EGYP

EGYPT POCKET GUIDE

Alberto Siliotti

THE AMERICAN UNIVERSITY IN CAIRO PRESS

Text and Photographs Alberto Siliotti
Drawings Stefania Cossu,
         Elisa Martini

General Editing Yvonne Marzoni
Graphic Design Geodia Edizioni
English Translation Cristina Alesii

This edition first published in Egypt jointly by
The American University in Cairo Press (Cairo and New York)
Elias Modern Publishing House (Cairo)
Geodia (Verona, Italy)

Created by Geodia (Verona, Italy)
Printed in Egypt by Elias Modern Publishing House (Cairo)
Distributed by the American University in Cairo Press (Cairo and New York)

Contents

The Church of al-Mu'allaqa, Cairo

*The Monastery of the Syrians
(Wadi al-Natrun)*

COPTIC CAIRO   14

THE MONASTERIES OF WADI AL-NATRUN   30

THE MONASTERIES OF THE RED SEA   40

BIBLIOGRAPHY   48

CHRONOLOGY

2nd cent. BC	Hieroglyphs start being transcribed using the Greek alphabet; the Coptic script is born.
30 BC	Egypt becomes a province of the Roman Empire.
AD 48	St. Mark the Evangelist introduces Christianity to Egypt.
202	Emperor Septimius Severus' first major persecution of the Copts.
249	Persecution of the Copts continues under the reign of Decius.
284	Emperor Diocletian ascends to the throne, intensifying the persecutions started by his predecessors. Birth of the Coptic calendar.
313	Emperor Constantine the Great declares freedom of worship within the Roman Empire with the Edict of Milan. Persecution of the Christians stopped. The first churches are built.
324	Byzantium becomes capital of the Byzantine Empire, with the name of Constantinople.
330	Establishment of the first monastic communities.
350	The Bible is translated for the first time into the Coptic language.
380	Emperor Theodosius I, the Great, declares Christianity the official religion of the Byzantine Empire and bans all pagan cults (Edict of Thessalonica).
391	Patriarch Theophilus orders the destruction of the great pagan monuments of Alexandria.
394	Last hieroglyphic inscriptions at Philae.
451	The Council of Chalcedon asserts the double nature of Jesus, that of being fully human and fully divine. The Copts reject this dogma and split from the Roman Church.
476	End of the Western Roman Empire.
527	Emperor Justinian reorganizes the Eastern Roman Empire or 'Byzantine Empire.'
570	Birth of Prophet Muhammad.
619 – 629	Persian occupation of Egypt and destruction of many monasteries.
622	Muhammad escapes from Mecca to Medina (the *Hijra*).
641	Arab conquest of Egypt.
707	The use of the Coptic language in public documents is forbidden.
1517	Egypt becomes a province of the Ottoman Empire.
1798	Napoleon Bonaparte conquers Egypt.
1801 – 1914	Egypt is reintegrated into the Ottoman Empire by Muhammad 'Ali Pasha and his descendants.
1882	Britain's occupation of Egypt.
1910	Inauguration of the Coptic Museum.
1922	End of the British protectorate.

The Copts

The Copts are the Christians of Egypt, a community of over five million people that proudly preserves its traditions, calendar, and liturgy.

St. Mark the Apostle, founder of the church of Egypt

A Coptic religious festivity

Saint Mark the Evangelist, according to tradition, arrived in Alexandria, Egypt, around AD 48. His preaching soon made many converts among the population, the vast majority of whom eventually embraced the new faith.

At that time the local natives were known as *Aegyptioi*, from the toponym *Aegyptos*, which is the name that Greeks used to indicate the land of the Pharaohs (conquered by Alexander the Great in 332 BC), and is derived from the ancient name of the capital Memphis, *Het-ka-Ptah*, 'the house of the

soul of Ptah,' the main deity of the pantheon of Memphis. When the Arabs conquered Egypt in AD 641 the name *Aegyptioi* was transcribed in the

Arabic alphabet, which lacks vowels and the letter 'p.' The word thus turned into *Qbt*, pronounced *qibt*, from where the word 'Copt' is derived, and was

The arrival of the Apostle Mark in Alexandria of Egypt as depicted in one of the mosaics of the Basilica of Venice, which is dedicated to him

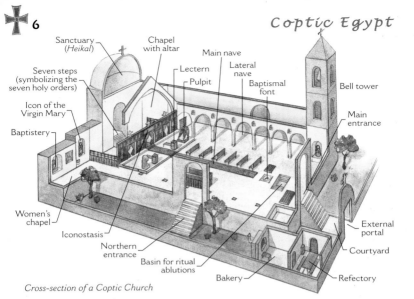

Cross-section of a Coptic Church

Labels: Sanctuary (*Heikal*); Chapel with altar; Main nave; Lateral nave; Lectern; Pulpit; Baptismal font; Seven steps (symbolizing the seven holy orders); Bell tower; Icon of the Virgin Mary; Main entrance; Baptistery; Women's chapel; Iconostasis; Northern entrance; Basin for ritual ablutions; Bakery; External portal; Courtyard; Refectory

His Holiness Pope Shenouda III, head of the Egyptian Coptic Orthodox Church

from then on used to indicate the local population of Christian faith. During the 2nd century, Christianity was already widespread, and the 4th to the 10th centuries witnessed the construction of a large number of monasteries, and churches, whose architectural structure follows specific canons derived from the requirements of the liturgy.

The main characteristic of the Coptic churches is the presence of the *iconostasis*, a decorated wooden wall that separates the nave, where worshippers stand, from the sanctuary.

Today the Copts, who split from the official Church in AD 453, after the Council of Chalcedon, form a community of over five million believers with their own church, the **Coptic Orthodox Church of Egypt**, headed since 1971 by H.H. Pope Shenouda III, the 117th successor of St. Mark, and Patriarch of Alexandria.

THE COPTIC CALENDAR

The Copts use a calendar, based on the pharaonic calendar created during the Ptolemaic period, which is the oldest still in use in the world: it represents a major element of cultural identity.

Since the 4th century, the Copts have adopted AD 284, the year marked by major religious persecutions launched by Emperor Diocletian, as the beginning of the 'Coptic Era,' or 'Era of Martyrs.'

The Coptic year starts on the first day of the month of Tut (September 11 of the Gregorian calendar), and has twelve months of thirty days, each of them connected to a pagan festivity or deity. At the end of the year a thirteenth month of five days, called 'intercalary month,' is added.

The other months are: Babah, Hatur, Kiahk, Tubah, Amshir, Barmahat, Barmudah, Bhasons, Baunah, Abib, Misra, and Nasi. The latest goes from September 6–10.

THE COPTIC LANGUAGE

The Coptic language is the direct descendant of the language spoken by the Egyptians since the time of the pharaohs.

*The **Coptic alphabet** represents the last stage of the hieroglyphic and subsequent demotic script under the influence of Greek script.*

Around the 2nd century BC, the Egyptians

Nom Hieroglyphique determiné	en lettres coptes	Mot Copte
	CШNT (П.)	ПⲤⲬⲈⲚⲦ(ⲉⲙ.ⲣ
	ⲦШⲢ·Ⲧ.	ⲦⲢⲈⲘ
	ОⲦⲨ.	. . . . .
	ⲦШ·ⲐШ	(ⲐШϢ·ⲦШϢ)
	ⲦОⲨⲦ	ⲦⲨⲨШⲦ
	ⲚⲠⲢⲈ	ⲚⲀⲠⲢⲈ
	ⲔⲖⲤ·ⲔⲢⲤ	. . . . . .

A page from the Egyptian grammar book used by Jean-François Champollion, who made use of his knowledge of the Coptic language to decipher the hieroglyphic script

THE COPTIC ALPHABET

ⲗ	a	Ⲡ	p
Ⲃ	b,v	Ⲣ	r
Ⲅ	g,gh	Ⲥ	s
Ⲇ	d,th	Ⲧ	t,d
Ⲉ	e	Ⲩ	u,y
Ⲋ	s	Ⲫ	f
Ⲍ	z	Ⲭ	k,kh
Ⲏ	ee	Ⲯ	ps
Ⲑ	th,t	Ⲱ	o (long)
Ⲓ	i	ϣ	sh
Ⲕ	k	ϥ	f
ⲗ	l	ϧ	kh
Ⲙ	m	ϩ	h
Ⲛ	n	ϫ	g,j
Ⲝ	x	ϭ	ch
Ⲟ	o	ϯ	tee

The Coptic alphabet derives from the Greek: in red are the additional letters taken from demotic

The tools of a Coptic scribe

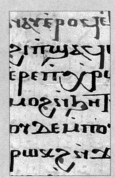

started transcribing their language using the Greek alphabet because of its simplicity.

To the Greek letters they added other phonemes taken from the demotic alphabet, which denoted specific sounds.

In the 1st century AD, the new script was already widely used.

Unlike the hieroglyphic script, the Coptic alphabet uses vowels, and letters have only a phonetic value.

The Coptic language included more than ten regional dialects, of which two were the main ones: the Sahidic in Upper Egypt, and the Bohairic in the Lower Egypt, which eventually became the dominant language in the 10th century.

The Coptic language was the symbol of a cultural identity and can be considered the oldest language still spoken in the world. It was commonly spoken until the 16th century and afterward used in the liturgical services. Around the 5th century a real Coptic literature, with texts of religious, hagiographic, and didactical contents started flourishing.

An example of Coptic script

The Itinerary of the Holy Family

*R*ich oral traditions and some apocryphal texts
blending religious faith and popular beliefs
have conveyed the story of the Flight to Egypt of
the Holy Family.

Icon showing the Flight of the Holy Family to Egypt

The Gospel according
to Matthew narrates
that the Holy Family, after
receiving the order from
an angel, leaves Palestine
and seeks refuge in Egypt
for three years to
protect Jesus from the
persecution of Herod the
Great, king of Judea
(Matthew, II, 13–23).

Yet there is no
historical record of this
journey. We only have a
mixture of oral traditions
based on an apocryphal
gospel, known as the
Apocryphal Gospel of
Pseudo-Matthew, and on a

book entitled *Vision of
Theophilus*, written
during the 4th century
by Theophilus, the 23rd

patriarch of Alexandria.

Through the centuries
the deep religiosity of the
Copts strengthened the
story, to the point where
the Flight to Egypt is now
an important element of
popular faith. The places
visited by the Holy Family
according to tradition
became places of worship
where churches and
monasteries were built.

The Holy Family,
whose arrival in Egypt is
celebrated on the June 1,
followed an itinerary
along the Mediterranean
coast of the Sinai,
stopping first at the
ancient city of **Farma**
(**Pelusium**), considered
the 'Door to Egypt,' on
the caravan road linking
Egypt to Syria and
Palestine, and continuing
to **Basta**, near present-

The ruins of Pelusium, ancient Farma

The 'Tree of the Virgin Mary' at Matariya: the present plant is from year 1672, and replaces the old one, which died

day Zagazig. From here, the Holy Family headed to **Musturud** and then **Sakha**, between Damietta and Rosetta, entering the **desert of Scetis**, known today as Wadi al-Natrun, and finally reaching **Matariya**.

This village, now a suburb of Cairo, is situated quite close to the ruins of Heliopolis, the sacred city of the sun god Re-Harakhti, and one of the most important religious centers of Ancient Egypt. Only a few remains and a beautiful obelisk built by Sesostris I (1964–1919 BC) are left of the city.

At Matariya is a giant

The obelisk of Sesostris I at Heliopolis

sycamore that tradition indicates is the tree under which the Holy Family rested. Situated at the center of a small garden, the plant is believed to have sprung in the place where the Virgin Mary threw away the water used to bathe and freshen up the child Jesus. After Matariya, the Holy Family headed toward **Zeituna**, another suburb of Cairo, where a basilica dedicated to the Virgin Mary was built and where there was a miraculous apparition of the Virgin in 1968.

From here, the Holy Family moved to the **Fortress of Babylon**, today the oldest district of Cairo, where the Virgin Mary and child Jesus lived in a cave upon which the Church of St. Sergius was built. The cave is believed to be close to the

The entrance to the Church of St. Sergius in Old Cairo

The Basilica of the Virgin Mary at Zeituna

The Church of the Virgin Mary in Maadi, built on the place where, according to tradition, the Holy Family embarked on the journey to Upper Egypt

riverbank where Moses, abandoned to the waters of the Nile, was found and saved, in the place marked today by a synagogue.

After their stay in the cave at Babylon, the Holy Family reached present-day **Maadi**, in the southern outskirts of Cairo, where it embarked on its journey to Upper Egypt. On the site of the embarkment stands a large church dedicated to the Virgin Mary. In 1976, some

Fishermen by the banks of the Nile at Maadi, near to the spot where the Holy Family embarked on their journey to Upper Egypt

monks recovered a perfectly preserved Bible (kept today in the same church) floating on

the waters of the Nile and open to the page of Psalm 19:2 of Prophet Isaias: 'Blessed shall be my people, Egypt.'

From Maadi, the Holy Family sailed southward to Samalut, disembarking by **Gebel al-Tayr**, 'the Mountain of the birds.' The Holy Family spent time in a cave upon which Helena, mother of Emperor Constantine the Great, ordered the building of the monastery of Deir al-Adhra, dedicated to the Virgin Mary.

After the stop at Gebel al-Tayr, the Holy Family continued the journey, crossing the

The Monastery of Deir al-Adhra at Gebel al-Tayr

The remains of the great Basilica of al-Ashmunein

Icon showing the Virgin Mary with Jesus in the Church of al-Muharraq

Nile to reach Hermopolis Magna, present-day **al-Ashmunein**, a city which at the time of the pharaohs was sacred to the god Thoth. The most important existing remains are those of a Christian basilica probably dedicated to the Virgin.

After stopping briefly by the villages of **Meir** and **al-Qusiya**, the Holy Family headed toward what is today the Monastery of **al-Muharraq**, north of Asyut, the ancient Lycopolis, where according to tradition,

the Holy Family spent over six months, hence the name given to this place: 'second Bethlehem.' It was here, as recorded in the Gospel of Matthew, that Joseph received the order from an angel to return to Judea as the 'danger had ceased' (Matthew, II, 19–21), obviously implying that Herod was dead.

According to tradition, before starting the journey back to Palestine, the Holy Family stopped at **Gebel Durunka**, a few kilometers south of Asyut, where a monastery, center of a very important

Interior of the Church of al-Muharraq

pilgrimage during the month of August, is now situated.

It is believed that this was the southernmost spot reached by the Holy Family during the journey in Egypt.

The Monastery of al-Muharraq, north of Asyut

Monks and Hermits

*T*he desert was the place chosen by the first Christians to get closer to God, and from the 3rd century on, monks, hermits, and anchorites came here to pray and meditate in solitude.

The first monastic centers rose during the 4th century in the desert west of the Delta

I t was in AD 330 that the monks Amoun and Macarius the Great founded the first monastic communities of Egypt, respectively at **Nitria** and **Scetis**, present day Wadi al-Natrun. A few years later, in 338, Amoun founded a third monastic center called **Kellia**, 'the cells,' situated at around ten kilometers south of Nitria.

Both monks were inspired by St. Antony 251–356), St. Paul of Thebes (228–348), and St. Pachomius (292–346), considered to be the founding fathers of Egyptian monasticism

St. Antony (left) and St. Paul of Thebes (right), founders of monasticism in the 4th century (Cairo, Coptic Museum

St. Pachomius (292–346), founder of cenobitism

the archaeological excavations conducted at Kellia, discovered in 1964, have unearthed over 1,500 individual hermitages spread over an area of one hundred square kilometers and grouped in different complexes: the ones of Qusur al-Izayla and Qusur al-Rubayyat flourished during the 7th century and are the most important.

The research has enabled scholars to reconstruct the life and the customs of the fathers of the desert who lived here until the 8th century.

although with different paths: anchoritism (total individual isolation in the desert), in Antony and Paul; cenobitism (communal isolation) in Pachomius.

While there are no remains at all of Nitria due to agricultural development in the area,

Aerial view of some hermitages at Kellia

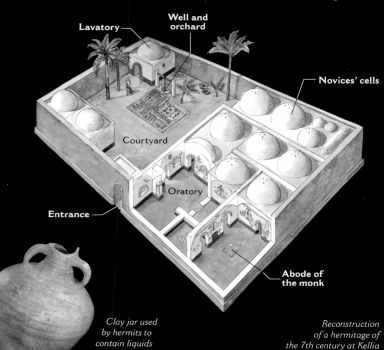

Lavatory

Well and orchard

Novices' cells

Courtyard

Oratory

Entrance

Abode of the monk

Clay jar used by hermits to contain liquids

Reconstruction of a hermitage of the 7th century at Kellia

Coptic Cairo

*I*nside the walls of the ancient Roman fortress of Babylon lived the original nucleus of the Coptic community of Cairo.

Religious crafts

One of the narrow street of Coptic Cairo

The so-called 'Coptic Cairo' corresponds to the historical part of the city known as 'Old Cairo' (*Misr al-Qadima*) or *Qasr al-Sham'a* ('Fortress of the candle') which occupied a part of the Roman fortress of Babylon in Egypt. This toponym of still obscure origins was probably related to the ancient Egyptian name *per-Hapi-en-On* ('the house of the Nile of On') used to indicate *Heliopolis*.

The fortress was built around the year 30 BC on the remains of a Persian fort of the 7th century BC raised to secure the protection of ancient capital *Memphis* and to control navigation on the Nile. The fortress was rebuilt

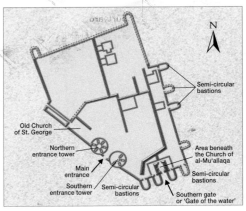

Plan of the ancient fortress of Babylon in Egypt

A semi-circular bastion that is part of the ramparts of the fortress of Babylon

are two circular towers that flanked its original entrance: the northern one, which was totally rebuilt, has been encompassed in the Greek-Orthodox Church of St. George (*Mari Girgis*, not to be confused with the nearby Coptic-Orthodox Nunnery of St. George, also called *Deir al-Banat*, 'monastery of the women'); the southern tower, partially demolished, flanks the entrance of the current Coptic Museum.

On the southwestern side of the ancient fortress, part of the

and enlarged in the 2nd century AD under the reign of Trajan (98–117), in a period when the Nile used to flow nearby, thus guarantee-ing a supply of water.

The fortress offered refuge to the local Christian population and during the 4th century the very first church of the city, the Church of al-Mu'allaqa or 'the hanging Church,' was built on the site.'

What remains of the ancient Roman fortress

The remains of the southern entrance tower of the fortress of Babylon, 1st century AD

original Roman ramparts made of bricks and two semi-circular bastions that frame the southern entrance called 'Gate of the water' are visible.

The perfectly preserved eastern bastion encloses the chapel of St. Takla Haymanut, the patron saint of Ethiopia, and it is part of the Church of al-Mu'allaqa.

The renovated northern entrance tower is now part of the Greek-Orthodox Chruch of St. George (Mari Girgis)

AL-FUSTAT

Immediately north and east of Old Cairo is a large area known as al-Fustat, Arabic for 'the tents.'

This was the place where 'Amr ibn al-'As, the Arab commander who in AD 641 invaded and conquered Egypt, installed his headquarters, which later on became the capital of the country.

However, the new master did not destroy the nearby fortress of Babylon, inhabited by the locals called 'Copts,' or 'the Egyptians,' and the two communities lived together for centuries without problems. Al-Fustat soon acquired growing importance as it flourished as a great city with richly decorated houses and bazaars selling products from as far away as China, and Spain, recorded al-Muqqadasi, the 10th-century Arab historian. But during the Fatimid period (969–1171) al-Fustat declined in importance, as a new capital called 'al-Qahira,' was being built slightly to the north and would become present-day Cairo. In 1168 al-Fustat was almost completely destroyed by a fire, and by the 14th century the place was reduced to a wasteland, which was used as a garbage dump during the entire Mamluk period (1250–1517). Today, al-Fustat is a large uncultivated wetland with a small lake called Ain al-Sira, from which some interesting ruins, water tanks, marble columns, foundations of ancient houses, and rests of thermal baths emerge as remains of a glorious past.

The first archaeological excavations in the area of al-Fustat, one of the most important sites of the Islamic period, started in 1912,

Some brick structures at the archaeological site of al-Fustat; in the foreground a water tank

At al-Fustat there are numerous marble columns from ancient buildings. In the background are the buildings of modern Cairo

The Al-Fustat Ceramics Center,
inaugurated in 2001

continued in 1970 thanks to the Egyptian Antiquities Department, and were resumed again in 1978 by the University of Waseda (Japan).

The searches have brought to light a huge number of finds that confirm the impressive wealth of the capital and its commercial bonds with China and the East.

Since the Mamluk period al-Fustat was a center for the production and manufacturing of pottery, and this tradition still exists today. There are in fact countless small handicraft workshops in present-day al-Fustat, producing all sorts of clay items; in 2001, under the supervision of the Ministry of Culture, a major center of development of artistic ceramics, called Al-Fustat Ceramics Center was inaugurated.

This center was designed by the Egyptian architect Gamal Amer and build over a 2,400 square meter-area: it includes a museum, spaces

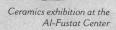

Ceramics exhibition at the
Al-Fustat Center

for temporary exhibitions, numerous ateliers for artists, and a specialized library with books about art and pottery.

Clay handicrafts from
al-Fustat area

Souk al-Fustat is a center created
to market the local handicrafts

The Last Supper on an icon of the Church of St. Sergius

The Church of St. Sergius

The majority of the oldest Coptic churches is to be found in the area of Old Cairo. The **Church of St. Sergius** (*Abu Sarga*), dedicated to Sts. Sergius and Bacchus, dates back to the early 5th century and has a structure of three naves separated by two rows of monolithic columns. St. Sergius is considered the oldest church in Egypt. It was built upon the cave, now transformed into a crypt, where according to tradition the Holy Family stayed for some time. The place, which today cannot be visited, was drained in 2003 from infiltration of water that flooded and damaged it.

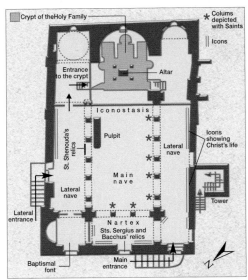

Plan of the Church of St. Sergius

THE SYNAGOGUE OF BEN EZRA

This synagogue, named after the Rabbi Ibrahim Ben Ezra who bought it in the 12th century, is the sole evidence of an important Hebrew community in al-Fustat.

The synagogue, which originally was a church, was built on the site where, according to tradition, Moses was found in the basket after being abandoned in the waters of the Nile.

The most famous rabbi of this place of worship was the great scientist Moises Ben Maimon (1135–1204), also known as 'Maimonides,' personal physician to Saladin. Restoration of the present-day building, which dates to 1892, was completed in 1995. The interior decoration and the furniture are from the late 19th century.

Icon depicting St. Barbara

12th century. It was built to house the relics of the saint, and according to the great Egyptian historian of the 14th century al-Maqrizi, it was the most beautiful church in Cairo.

The edifice has an architectural plan similar to that of the Church of St. Sergius, and can be considered a sister building. The fine wooden iconostasis with inlays in ivory is from the 13th century.

The **Church of St. Barbara** (*Sitt Barbara*), situated about a hundred meters eastward from the Church of St. Sergius, was built on the ruins of a 5th-century church dedicated to Sts. Cyrus and John, titulars nowadays of a chapel beside the church. St. Barbara, a martyr from Nicomedia in Asia Minor, lived between the 2nd and 4th century and was beheaded after she tried to convert her own father and the Roman governor.

The present-day church dates back to the

The central nave of the Church of St. Barbara

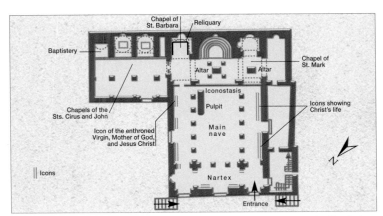

Plan of the Church of St. Barbara

The Church of al-Mu'allaqa

The façade of the Church of al-Mu'allaqa

*T*he most famous church of Coptic Cairo is known as 'the Hanging Church' (in Arabic, 'al-Mu'allaqa') and is dedicated to the Holy Virgin. Its name comes from the fact that it was built over one of the bastions of the fortress of Babylon.

A steep staircase leads to the most famed and revered church of Coptic Cairo, 'the Hanging Church.' The floor of the church is in fact 'suspended' at several meters over the street level, as the religious edifice stands on one of the semicircular bastions flaking the southern entrance of the fortress of Babylon.

It is believed that its construction took place in the 7th century, but the earliest references to this church are from the 9th century. In the 10th century the church was restored, then plundered under Caliph al-Hakim (996–1021) and finally, starting from the 11th century, it became the seat of the Patriarchate of Alexandria. The building underwent several renovations between the 17th and 19th centuries, which modified the original appearance and structure. After other restorations during the 20th century, the church acquired its present look.

The **entrance staircase** leads to an **external portico**, surmounted by a wooden frieze showing Jesus

The external portal of the Church of al-Mu'allaqa

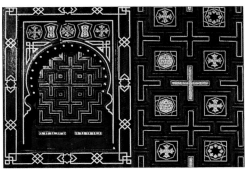

with **three internal naves**. The two lateral naves are separated from the central one by two ranks of eight columns each surmounted by Corinthian capitals probably originating from an older building.

The central nave is divided in two by a row of three columns.

The **iconostasis** made of cedar wood with inlays of ivory and ebony, dates

Detail of the iconostasis with its decorations

between two angels, which leads to an **aisle**.

The aisle opens onto an **internal courtyard**, and after a **second portico**, built in the 11th century, we find the church itself. Its structure is typical of the paleochristian churches,

Corinthian capital

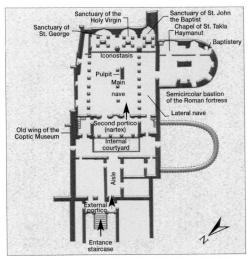

Plan of the Church of al-Mu'allaqa

Left side of the main nave of the Church of al-Mu'allaqa

Lunettes

Second portico and
entrance doors

Façade with carved
wooden frieze

Internal
courtyard

The Church of
al-Mu'allaqa

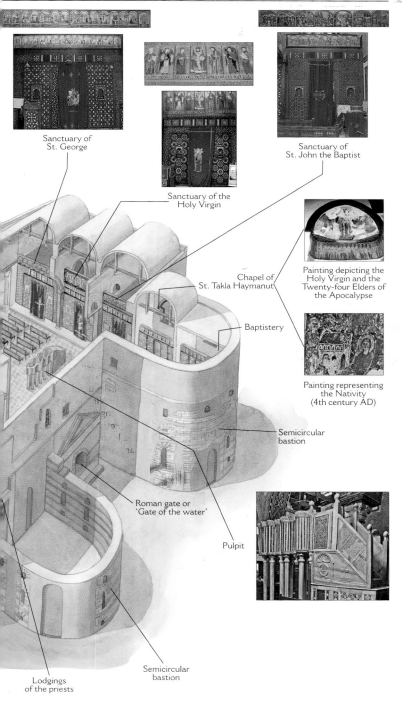

Sanctuary of
St. George

Sanctuary of the
Holy Virgin

Sanctuary of
St. John the Baptist

Chapel of
St. Takla Haymanut

Painting depicting the
Holy Virgin and the
Twenty-four Elders of
the Apocalypse

Baptistery

Painting representing
the Nativity
(4th century AD)

Semicircular
bastion

Roman gate or
'Gate of the water'

Pulpit

Semicircular
bastion

Lodgings
of the priests

The stairs of the pulpit and the panel carved with a double cross

The marble pulpit (or ambo) supported by fifteen columns

from the 14th century and is finely carved with elaborated geometrical motifs: its uppermost part bears 18th century icons. Those facing the central nave depict the enthroned Jesus flanked by the Virgin Mary, the archangel Gabriel and St. Peter on the left, and St. John the Baptist, the archangel Michael, and St. Paul on the right.

Behind the iconostasis are the **three sanctuaries** dedicated to the Holy Virgin in the middle, to St. George on the left, and to St. John the Baptist on the right. The iconostasis that separates the two lateral sanctuaries is also surmounted by icons depicting the lives of the two saints.

Between the first pair of columns dividing the central nave is a magnificent marble **pulpit** (or ambo) from the 11th century, resting on a series of fifteen

The sanctuary of the Holy Virgin in the central nave

church by a cedar panel, and is situated behind a finely carved door.

The wall decorations of the apse, dating from the 13th century, show the Holy Virgin surrounded by angels, while underneath are twenty-four bishops probably representing the Twenty-four Elders of the Apocalypse, part of the celestial court, and having priestly functions; another

The sanctuary of
St. John the Baptist

graceful columns symbolizing Jesus, the twelve apostles, and the two evangelists, St. Mark and St. Luke.

On both sides of the pulpit is a lateral panel carved with high-reliefs of a Coptic cross surmounted by a shell, and a second cross placed on a stylized Mount Calvary.

The lateral nave on the right communicates with one of the two semicircular bastions (the eastern one) flanking the southern gate ('the Gate of the water') of the ancient fortress of Babylon: inside the bastion is the **Chapel of St. Takla Haymanut**, the patron saint of

Ethiopia who lived in the 13th century.

The chapel, discovered during the restoration works made in 1984, is separated from the

painting of different style depicts instead the Nativity of Jesus Christ.

Beside the Chapel of St. Takla is a small baptismal font.

The apse of the Chapel of St. Takla Haymanut with the
Holy Virgin and the Twenty-four Elders of the Apocalypse

The Coptic Museum

*R*eopened to the public in June 2006 after a long restoration, the Coptic Museum displays the major masterpieces of Christian art in Egypt.

The façade of the Coptic Museum

*F*ounded in 1908 by Marcus Simaika Pasha (1864–1944), a Cairene notable and an art collector who also acted as its first curator, the Coptic Museum was inaugurated in March 1910, expanded several times, and is the most important museum in the world of Egyptian Christian art.

A stone plaque placed to the left of the entrance in 1947, during the reign of King Farouk I, recalls in Arabic, Coptic, and English the creation of the museum by Simaika, who for many years collected finds and valuable architectural items originating from private collections, churches, and palaces, saving from dispersion and destruction a unique and priceless artistic legacy.

A second plaque, close to the previous one, commemorates the reopening of the museum in June 2006 in the presence of

Capital from the Monastery of St. Jeremiah at Sakkara

Plaque commemorating the creation of the Coptic Museum

The founder of the Coptic Museum, Marcus Simaika Pasha

conducted during the 20th century, the collections of the Egyptian Museum, and the churches of Cairo.

In just a few decades the original structure of the museum, corresponding to the 'old wing,' was not enough to house all the finds, and in 1947 the museum was enlarged with the addition of a 'new wing.'

Twenty years later, in 1966, it was necessary to conduct the first restoration works, which lead to its closure until 1984.

The last overhauls in 1992 and 2006 have preserved the classical and unique character of the old museum along with the modern demands for conservation and display. The museum is divided into several

President Hosni Mubarak, following its closure in the aftermath of the 1992 earthquake.

The museum, situated next to the Church of al-Mu'allaqa, consists of two wings developing on two stories around two large courtyards used as exhibition areas.

The museum, which occupies an area of 8,000 square meters, gathers over 1,600 finds of Coptic art from numerous excavations

Detail of a lunette depicting Christ, from the Monastery of Bawit

View of the 'old wing' of the museum

Gravestone of the 7th–8th century with an inscription in Greek stating the name of the deceased, and two ankh crosses

sections. A large area is dedicated to the exhibition of **architectural finds** mainly from the Monastery of St. Jeremiah at Sakkara, which occupy the first courtyard, and masterpieces of the Copt sculpture—among these are funerary stelae, gravestones, friezes, reliefs, and other architectural elements dating from the 2nd to the 7th century, often showing pagan and pharaonic influences together with typically Christian motifs.

Wide space is given to

mural painting, a form of fundamental importance in the Coptic art, which flourished around the 7th century.

The majority of the finds comes from the Monasteries of St. Jeremiah at Sakkara

and St. Apollo at Bawit, one of the largest monasteries of Egypt founded north of Asyut in the 4th century, where excavations started by the French archaeologist Jean Clédat in 1900.

From Bawit, which witnessed great splendor during the 7th century and was later abandoned, come some of the most important finds of the museum, among which is a lunette depicting Jesus Christ inside a garland, and a big niche dating from the 6th or 7th century.

The latter shows, on the upper side, an image of the triumphant Christ, and below a depiction of an enthroned Virgin Mary with Jesus on her lap, surrounded by the Apostles (St. Peter can be seen to the right of Mary). In their hands the Apostles hold Gospels inside richly decorated cases.

An entire section of the museum is

Niche of the 7th–8th century representing an enthroned Christ (above) and the Virgin Mary holding Jesus, surrounded by the Apostles (below), both from the monastery of Bawit

dedicated to the production of writings, with over 700 precious illuminated **manuscripts and codices**, which include some of exceptional importance such as those written on papyrus and dating from the 4th century, found in Nag Hammadi (Upper Egypt) in 1945.

An invaluable manuscript with miniatures

A page of the codices of Nag Hammadi

various philosophical doctrines that have influenced Christianity since its inception.

Extremely rich are the **collection of icons**, most of them from the churches of Cairo and monasteries from all over Egypt; the **collection of wooden boxes** inlaid with silver and colored glass, made to contain the Gospels; the **collection of bronze lamps** of different shapes; and above all, the **collection of textiles**

that are one of the most typical products of the Coptic arts and crafts.

Copts mastered techniques of weaving and dyeing linen and later wool.

The oldest dyed fabrics and the first decorated tapestries date back from the 2nd to the 5th century, mixing geometrical, naturalistic, mythologic, and religious motifs with typical elements of the pagan iconography.

These codices of over 1,200 pages form a complete library and contain Gnostic treatises ('gnostic' is from the Greek *gnosis*, meaning 'knowledge') whose nature is heterogeneous.

They are mostly texts translated into the Coptic language from works written in Greek, but among them are also the earliest apocryphal Gospels known today, such as the 'Gospel of Thomas,' which is believed to quote the very words of Jesus.

The study of the texts of Nag Hammadi, not yet completed, is casting new light on the

Fabric woven with linen and wool, dating from the 4th–5th century, probably from Antinoe (present-day al-Sheikh Ibada)

The Monasteries of Wadi al-Natrun

This desert region with its unusual landscapes was famous for its salt in the Egypt of the pharaohs. It was also a land the Holy Family passed through and where the first communities of Christian ascetics were born.

One of the characteristic salty lakes of Wadi al-Natrun

Wadi al-Natrun is a desert depression located nearly ninety kilometers northwest of Cairo. The deepest part of the depression, which covers an area of a hundred square kilometers, is around twenty-three meters below sea level, and is occupied by a succession of salty and strongly alkaline lakes, where no life is found with the exception of micro-organisms that have adapted to this extreme habitat.

The level of these lakes varies depending on the season: it rises between December and March, and beginning in April the water evaporates almost completely due to the high temperatures.

The depression

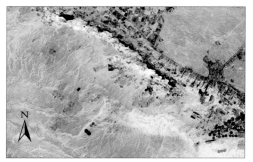

Satellite view of Wadi al-Natrun

possibly originates both from phenomena of wind erosion and from the actions of ancient river basins.

During the Quaternary Period, Wadi al-Natrun

Natron crystals

Tradition says the Holy Family crossed this inhospitable region en route to present-day Cairo. This was one of the reasons why many hermits and anchorites, beginning in the 4th century, choose this solitary desert area, which they found was ideal to becoming closer to God.

Wadi al-Natrun is home to four important monasteries, all still active: the monasteries of al-Baramous (in Arabic, *Baramus*), the Syrians (*al-Suryani*), St. Bishoi (*Anba Bishoi*) and St. Macarius (*Abu Makar*).

Each monastery (in Arabic, *deir*) is a self-contained entity, and is surrounded by vast green, well cultivated tracts of land that stand in contrast to the surrounding white wilderness.

Today the natron is still an important economic resource used in the production of glass and also textiles.

was a large lagoon by the edge of the Mediterranean Sea, and the region, called Nitria by the Greeks and Scetis by the Romans, was well-known in Ancient Egypt as it provided a salt, the *natron*, consisting of a mixture of bicarbonate and hydrate carbonate of sodium, and sulfate of sodium, which was the fundamental element in the embalming process.

The natron, extracted from deep mineralized strata, has in fact a very strong dehydrating power, and the bodies of the dead were covered in this substance for not less than forty days.

The monasteries of Wadi al-Natrun are small oasis of vegetation surrounded by a desert of salt

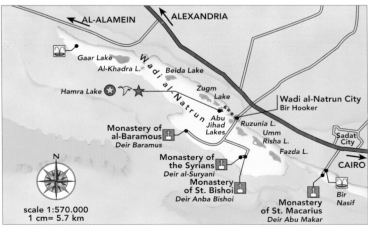

Map of Wadi al-Natrun

The Monastery of al-Baramous

*T*he Monastery of al-Baramous is the northernmost of the monasteries of Wadi al-Natrun and perhaps the oldest; it is believed to have been built on the place where St. Macarius the Great settled down in AD 330.

The imposing walls of the Monastery of al-Baramous date from the late 11th century

*T*he toponym 'Baramous' derives from the Coptic *Pa-Romeos* that means 'the two Romans.' According to tradition, it refers to Maximus and Domitius, sons of Emperor Valentinian I (364–375), who embraced the Christian faith, withdrew to pray in this desolate region, and were later sanctified.

They were welcomed by St. Macarius, founder of the monastery, where they were buried.

The religious complex underwent repeated attacks and pillaging throughout the

The modern bell towers of the monastery

The fortified keep of the 7th century

centuries, especially between the 5th and 9th century.

Today its oldest structure, the tower or keep or *qasr*, dates from the beginning of the 7th century.

In this tower, common to many monasteries and accessible only through a drawbridge, the monks used to retire to protect themselves from desert robbers.

The main church inside the complex is devoted to the Virgin Mary, and dates from the 11th century, but was built on the ruins of a pre-existing structure.

The church, which is considered the oldest at Wadi al-Natrun, has a classical plan with three naves and three different sanctuaries: under the altar of the main sanctuary are the remains of Sts. Maximus and Domitius, while on the southern wall of the main nave are paintings dating from the 13th–14th

centuries, inspired by episodes of the life of Jesus.

Painting of the church of the Virgin Mary depicting St. Michael

The Church of the Virgin Mary

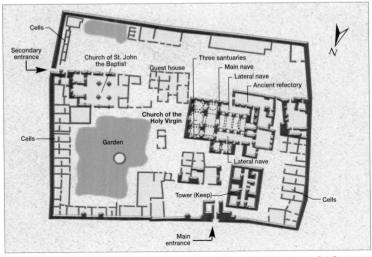

Plan of the Monastery of al-Baramous

The Monastery of the Syrians

*B*uilt on the site where St. Bishoi had a vision of Christ, this is the smallest of Wadi al-Natrun's monasteries, but the most artistically attractive, due to the beauty of its wall paintings.

The strong walls enclosing the Monastery of the Syrians date from the end of the 9th century and have an average height of around ten meters

The creation of this monastery, dedicated to the Virgin Mother of God (*Theotokos*) dates from the 7th century. It was built by a group of monks who left the Monastery of St. Bishoi (located five hundred meters away), after a theological dispute on the incorruptibility of the body of Christ (Jansenist heresy).

When at the beginning of the 8th century the dispute was resolved, the monks returned to their monastery of provenance: the new structure was purchased by a group of Syrian merchants and became the base of Syrian monks.

Later on, its abbot Moses of Nisibis gave the monastery

The Church of the Virgin Mary and the lodgings for the pilgrims

numerous Syrian manuscripts, as the first nucleus of a library which was to become one of the most important of the Coptic world and that now contains over 3,000 invaluable tomes. Starting from the 16th century, the monastery slowly opened to Egyptian monks as well, who eventually replaced the original occupants.

The monastery has a quite peculiar plan—being narrow and elongated—which supposedly recalls the shape of Noah's Ark.

The splendid fresco in Byzantine style, discovered in 1991 in the Church of the Holy Virgin, represents the Annunciation: Mary and the Angel of God are flanked by the prophets Moses and Isaias on the right, and Ezequiel and Daniel on the left

The magnificent wooden gate, called 'Gate of the Prophecies', in the Church dedicated to the Holy Vergin

Dating to the 7th century, the main church is dedicated to the Holy Virgin and has some of the most beautiful paintings of the Coptic art inspired by the highest moments of the life of the Holy Virgin Mary (Annunciation, Nativity, Ascension, and Dormition).

Under the scene that represents the Ascension a unique masterpiece of the Coptic art was discovered in 1991: a second Annunciation of Byzantine style dating to the 10th century, from the time of Moses of Nisibis. These paintings have been object of several studies and restorations, started in 1995 by an international team coordinated by the University of Leiden (The Netherlands).

Among the edifices of the monastery are the other three churches, the chapel of the forty-nine martyrs, the refectory, and the three-story fortified tower of the mid-9th century.

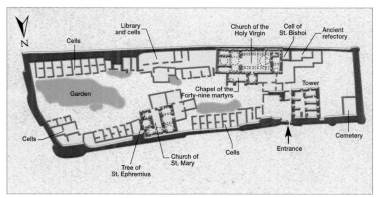

Plan of the Monastery of the Syrians

The Monastery of St. Bishoi

The Monastery of St. Bishoi was founded in the 5ᵗʰ century by the hermit monk Bishoi and destroyed several times by the Berbers. Today, it is the second residence of H.H. Pope Shenouda III.

General view of the Monastery of St. Bishoi

In 1981, President Anwar al-Sadat (1918–1981) legally confined the Coptic pope to the Monastery of St. Bishoi. He was released by President Hosni Mubarak four years later.

The Monastery of St. Bishoi (in Coptic *Anba Bishoi*, or more precisely *Pschoi*) was named after the monk who lived between 320 and 417, and whose name means 'the Elevated.' St. Bishoi retired and lived here for over forty years, founding an important community of anchorites. He later on left to retire in deeper solitude to a place where he had a vision of Christ, and where the Monastery of the Syrians was eventually built.

As with all the other monasteries at Wadi al-

The strong perimeter wall of the 9th century, and the entrance to the Monastery of St. Bishoi

Natrun, the Monastery of St. Bishoi was plundered and destroyed several times by desert robbers.

It was even ruined by termites in the 11th century. It was due to the enormous restoration work conducted by Patriarch Benjamin II during the 14th century that the monastery exists.

Today, nearly 150 monks live in this monastery, which gave to the Coptic Church two patriarchs, Gabriel VIII and Macarius III.

The main church is dedicated to St. Bishoi, founder of the monastery, whose grave is inside the church.

The plan of the edifice, dating to the 9th century, is quite complex and has Syrian influences, with three sanctuaries dedicated to St. Bishoi, the Virgin Mary, and St. John the Baptist; two choirs separated by a wooden panel with ivory inlays dating to the 14th century, and three chapels dedicated to the Patriarch St. Benjamin, St. George, and St. Apaskhiron.

The other structures of the monastery consist in the usual keep; the refectory (today used as a museum) occupied

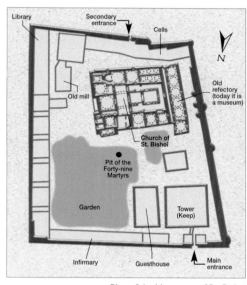

destruction during a siege by the Berbers in 1096. Its internal structure presents three stories: on the ground floor were the kitchens, on the first floor the abodes of the monks, now converted into a church, and on the third

Plan of the Monastery of St. Bishoi

almost entirely by a long and low masonry table; a millhouse and the Pit of the Forty-nine Martyrs, where according to tradition the Berbers washed their swords after killing the forty-nine martyrs in the Monastery of St. Macarius in 444.

The keep, or fortified tower, situated near the entrance gate of the walls, is the oldest and most interesting part of the religious complex. It owes its present appearance to the restoration work conducted in the 13th century after its

floor a chapel dedicated to the Archangel Michael, with valuable icons from the 18th century.

The old mill

Icon showing St. Bishoi

The Monastery of St. Macarius

St. Macarius the Great

Tucked away in a secluded corner far from the other monasteries of Wadi al-Natrun, the Monastery of St. Macarius is not well known or frequently visited.

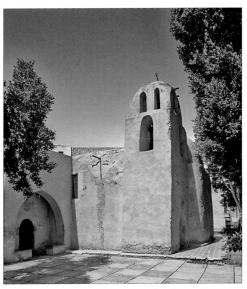

The chapel of the forty-nine martyrs

The Monastery of St. Macarius (in Arabic, *Deir Abu Maqar*) is the southernmost and largest house of worship in the area, but also less visited by tourists, who wrongly tend to ignore it.

The majority of the imposing structures presently observable is modern: in order to lodge the over one hundred monks that live here in total autonomy and at the same time host the numerous Coptic visitors, the complex needed major expansions that have made the monastery six times larger than the original.

The monastery, which has its own hospital, pharmacy, and even a modern print shop, is organized as a farm, where nearly 900 people work to meet the needs of the religious community.

After entering the complex through the entrance gate recently opened on the northern

The current structure of the Monastery of St. Macarius

side of the external walls (the original entrance was on the eastern side) and going through a 7th-century arch, visitors descend to the heart of the oldest part of the monastery, which includes the Church of St. Macarius, the Chapel of the Forty-nine Martyrs, the Church of St. Apaskhiron, the majestic tower or keep, the old refectory, and the monks' old cells.

St. Macarius, who along with St. Antony and St. Pachomius founded monasticism in Egypt, retired to the desert of Scetis around year 330, settling in the area now occupied by the Monastery of Baramous.

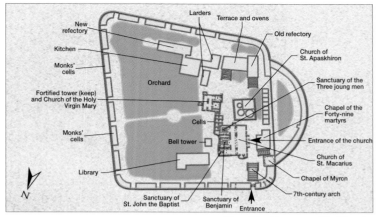

Plan of the Monastery of St. Macarius

Later, he decided to further seclude himself and moved south, where the monastery dedicated to him, is today.

Founded in the 4th century, such monastery suffered several attacks from the Berbers—the most famous is that of year 444, which ended with the killing of forty-nine monks

Macariuses') and has on its eastern side three sanctuaries with painted decorations of major importance: the first one with evident Fatimid influences, is dedicated to Sts. John the Baptist and Mark, and the second one to Patriarch Benjamin.

In the latter are some very rare images of the

Tetramorph (symbol of Christ and the four evangelists) painted on wood and dating from the 7th century.

The keep of the monastery dates back from the 5th century

The Tetramorph in the sanctuary of Benjamin

who refused to seek protection in the keep.

The Church of St. Macarius dates from 360, but its present appearance is due to several subsequent enlargements.

The church houses the relics of St. Macarius the Great, St. Macarius of Alexandria, and St. Macarius Bishop (the so-called 'Three

The sanctuary of Sts. John the Baptist and Mark, 7th century. The scene represents the sacrifice of Ibrahim

The Monasteries of the Red Sea

The Eastern Desert, to the west of the Egyptian coast of the Red Sea, was the place chosen by St. Antony, founder of monasticism, to escape the world and reach closeness to God in solitude.

The monastery of St. Antony and, in the background, the mountain and the cave where the saint lived

Around AD 270 Antony, who would be later venerated as 'St. Antony the Great' (251–356), decided to retire to the Eastern Desert and live in solitude and contemplation. He chose to dwell in a cave by a mountain, becoming the first monk (from the Greek *monos*, 'lonely') and anchorite (from the Greek *anakoreutes*, 'he who retires').

St. Macarius and St. Paul of Thebes choose to retire respectively to the desert of Scetis (now Wadi al-Natrun) and to the mountains that run along the coast of the Red Sea, where St. Paul lived in isolation for eighty years. It was

St. Antony the Great (251–356)

only during the middle of the 4th century that the monks abandoned the caves and started building the first monasteries.

A monk of the desert

The Monastery of St. Paul

*S*ituated at the end of a valley cutting through a mountain, the Monastery of St Paul was built upon the cave where St. Paul, the first hermit, lived.

St. Paul of Thebes (228–348)

General view of the monastery, whose origins date from the 5th century

St. Paul of Thebes, also known as 'St. Paul the Hermit,' was born in 228 to a family of rich merchants.

At the age of sixteen he withdrew to a valley of the Eastern Desert, situated around fifteen kilometers from the coast of the Red Sea, southwest of present-day Zafarana.

Dressed with a tunic made of palm leaves, St. Paul, who is considered the first hermit (he actually preceded his friend St. Antony), chose to dwell in a cave where tradition says he lived for over eighty years, eating only half a loaf of bread a day brought to him by a raven. Upon this cave, still visible, the monastery dedicated to him and called *Deir Mar Bulos* was built.

Despite the imposing walls that surround it, giving it the appearance of a fortress, the monastery was destroyed in 1484 during one of the numerous assaults of the Bedouins.

Entrance of the monastery

The Saint Knights depicted in the 13th century on the dome of the narthex

The church was subsequently enlarged to the north with the addition of another two sanctuaries dedicated to St. Antony and the Twenty-four Elders of the Apocalypse, a central nave, and of a narthex, or portico, where the entrance is now situated.

Its dome, also called 'dome of the Martyrs,' is decorated with the images of the 'Saint Knights' riding horses: St. James, St. Mena, St. Julius, St. Apater, St. Isidore,

A good part of the current buildings date to the 18th century when it was rebuilt (1701) and occupied by a group of monks from the nearby Monastery of St. Antony, which has managed it until 1974.

The heart of the monastery is the Church of St. Paul: its oldest and most attractive part is the sanctuary of St. Paul, which occupies the rocky cave where, according to tradition, the saint withdrew.

The sanctuary of St. Paul is the oldest part of the church

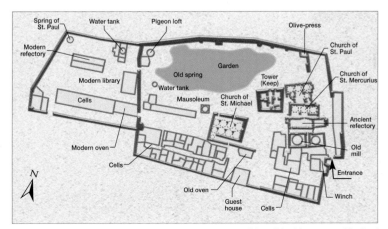

Plan of the Monastery of St. Paul

The old refectory with the long masonry table

and St. Apaskhiron. The walls and the vaults of the various domes in the church of St. Paul are decorated with rare mural paintings that mostly date from the 18th century.

The other two churches of the monastery, both dating from the 18th century, are dedicated to St. Michael (*al-Malak*) and St. Mercurius (*Abu Saifain*).

The former, which is the biggest of the complex and is today commonly used for the liturgical services, has a ceiling of twelve domes. The second church is built directly upon the Church of St. Paul, and linked to the latter by a staircase dug out of the rock.

The most imposing structure inside the monastery is the massive defensive tower or keep situated by the Church of St. Paul.

Originally, in the ground level of this building was the cemetery, while the second floor was used to store provisions to survive the sieges.

On the third floor was a chapel dedicated to the Virgin Mary, together with some cells where the monks could live when barricaded in. Contiguous to the Church of St. Paul is the old refectory dating from the 9th–10th century, with a vaulted ceiling; in it one can see a long and low masonry table where monks laid dishes and meals.

Nearby are two rooms with a mill and a big grindstone.

In the northeastern part of the monastery is the 'spring of St. Paul,' the main water supply of the monastery, which provides four cubic meters of water per day, still necessary today in the life of this community.

A second spring, called *Pool of Miriam*, is located to the south outside the monastery.

The garden of the monastery

The Monastery of St. Antony

*N*estled among the mountains in the wilderness, a few dozen kilometers from the Monastery of St. Paul, is the oldest and biggest of the Coptic monasteries.

*St. Antony the Great
(251–356)*

General view of the Monastery of St. Antony, founded during the 4th century

The Monastery of St. Antony (*Deir Anba Antunyus*) was founded in the 4th century by his disciples on the site of his grave, immediately after his death.

St. Antony the Great (251–356), also called 'St. Antony Abbot' or 'St. Antony of Egypt,' founder of monasticism in Egypt, withdrew to live in solitude in the desert in the year 270 at the age of nineteen. He lived in a cave 680 meters high, on the side of Gebel Qulzum, the mountain to the east of the monastery.

A steep staircase, two kilometers in length, now links the monastery to the cave.

The monastery is located more to the northeast than that of St. Paul, which is situated at about eighty kilometers by the paved road, but is much closer using the ancient trail that directly connects the two monastic complexes across the mountain. In spite of the isolation and tranquility of the area, the monastery had quite an eventful history.

It suffered attacks and plundering by the Bedouins during the 8th and the 9th century, and was pillaged by the Arabs in the 11th century. During the 15th century it suffered a gory rebellion by the Bedouin servants who slaughtered the

Bell towers of the monastery

Entrance gate with the hoist used in the past to access the monastery

The old hoist

monks and plundered the edifice.

The monastery was restored during the following century, and Syrian monks from Wadi al-Natrun settled there.

Preceded by a modern gate flanked by two tall white bell towers is the imposing ten-meter high wall, which surrounds the grounds of the monastery and the adjoining structures spread over an area of 60,000 square meters. Originally there was no entrance gate and the access was only through a hoist, perfectly preserved to the present day, which lifted monks and pilgrims inside a crate to the top of the walls.

Inside the walls thrived a totally self-contained village that consisted not only of numerous

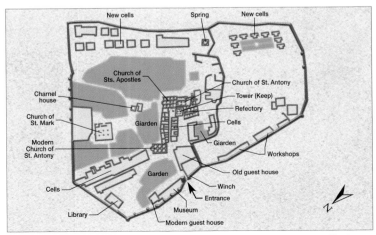

Plan of the monastery of St. Antony

The Church of St. Antony with the two big modern bell towers

churches, lodgings, and the usual defensive keep, but also enjoyed orchards, gardens, fruit gardens, warehouses, a millhouse, a library (which today preserves over 1,600 manuscripts), and a perennial spring that still provides 100 cubic meters of drinking water per day, guaranteeing a continuous vital water supply. Between the 17th and the 19th century the relevance of the

The monastery, with its keep, has a complex internal organization that guarantees a total autonomy

The central nave of the Church of St. Antony

monastery grew to the point that twelve patriarchs of the Coptic Church were elected among the monks of St. Antony.

The oldest and most important of the five churches of the monastery is the one dedicated to St. Antony, built upon the grave of the saint in the 4th century, and famed because of its beautiful mural paintings dating from the 13th century.

The ceiling of the choir

The wall-paintings of the church of St. Antony date back from the 13th century: most of them are by a monk called Theodore who worked in the church between 1232 and 1233. Distributed on the walls and the domes of the church, they represent the most complete cycle of all Coptic painting art. The iconographic program includes depictions of the Saint Knights, the Holy Virgin, Christ, the Prophets, and the most famous saints of Egypt.

The three sanctuaries of the church, dedicated to St. Antony (center), St. Athanasius (right,) and St. Mark (left), are decorated with scenes from the Old Testament and with a big Christ *Pantocrator* (Lord of the

Enthroned Christ and the Holy Virgin with Jesus in the central sanctuary

universe) that towers from the central sanctuary of St. Antony.

The paintings have undergone a restoration campaign started in 1999 and promoted by the Supreme Council of Antiquities (SCA) in cooperation with the American Research Center in Egypt (ARCE). The restoration program, which ended in 2001, has been conducted by an Italian team of specialists directed by Paolo and Laura Mora.

*Christ **Pantocrator** (Lord of the universe) in the central sanctuary*

BIBLIOGRAPHY

Bolman, E., (edited by) *Monastic Visions*, Cairo, 2002.

Buttler, A.J., *The Ancient Coptic Churches of Egypt*, Oxford, 1884.

Capuani, M., et alii, *Christian Egypt – Coptic Art and Monuments Through Two Millennia*, Cairo, 2002.

Gabra, G., (edited by) *Be Thou There – The Holy Family's Journey in Egypt*, Cairo, 2001.

Gabra, G., *Coptic Monasteries – Egypt's Monastic Art and Architecture*, Cairo, 2002.

Gabra, G., and Eaton-Krauss, M., *The Treasures of Coptic Art in the Coptic Museum and Churchus of Old Cairo*, Cairo, 2006.

Gabra, G., and Eaton-Krauss, M., *The Illustrated Guide to the Coptic Museum and Churches of Old Cairo*, Cairo, 2007.

Meinardus, O.F.A., *Monks and Monasteries of the Egyptian Deserts*, Cairo, 1961.

Meinardus, O.F.A., *The Holy Family in Egypt*, Cairo, 1986

Meinardus, O.F.A., *Coptic Saints and Pilgrimages*, Cairo, 2002.

*Detail of the Gate of the Prophecies
of the Monastery of the Syrians at Wadi al-Natrun*

PHOTOGRAPH CREDITS

DRAWINGS